Virtual Libraries

ıns

ɔr

organisations

Edited by Lewis Foreman
Librarian
Foreign & Commonwealth Office

CIRCLE OF STATE LIBRARIANS CSL

London: The Stationery Office
1997

STATE LIBRARIAN: Journal of the Circle of State Librarians
Editor: Lewis Foreman **November 1996**
Vol 42 no 3.

The last issue of *State Librarian* to appear in the long-familiar A4 yellow cover was Vol 39 No 3. Since then the journal has divided into two components: a series of monographs on specific themes published by HMSO, and "News and Views" distributed to members by the CSL, but not available to non-members. We apologise if this has caused any confusion.

The issues published by HMSO under these arrangements were:

Developing Quality in Libraries (March 1992)
ISBN 0 11 887537 X (Out of Print—photocopy service available)

Developing Professionals in Information Work (July/Nov 1992)
ISBN 0 11 887539 6

Change in Libraries and Information Services (March 1993)
ISBN 0 11 887542 6

Performance and Potential of Librarians edited by Linda Kerr
(July 1993) ISBN 0 11 887543 4

Market Testing and After (Nov 1993)
ISBN 0 11 887545 0

Networking and Libraries edited by Stephen Latham (Nov 1994)
ISBN 0 11 887547 7

Who Needs Libraries? (Oct 1995)
ISBN 0 11 887548 5

All back issues up to and including July 1993 are priced at £6.95. From Nov 1993 at £7.95. Orders should be placed with The Stationery Office. If you wish to place a Standing Order for future titles please write to: The Stationery Office, PO Box 276, London SW8 5DT or telephone 0171 873 8466 (fax 0171 873 8222), quoting Standing Order Classification reference 20–09–011.

ISBN 0 11 887550 7 ISSN 0305–9189

Contents

Contributors

Liz MacLachlan's varied career in government libraries has included the Royal College of Defence Studies, the ODA/FCO, Central Veterinary Laboratory and the Department of Trade and Industry, where she is Information Management Co-ordinator.

Ray Lester started as a clinical biochemist and subsequently a systems analyst. After the libraries of Bradford University and University College London, he became Librarian of the London Business School where his responsibilities encompassed computing, networking, audio-visual and library services. He has recently become Head of Library and Information Services at the Natural History Museum.

Liz Orna, Orna Stevens Associates, is an independent information consultant at present carrying out research on the role of information products and information in organisations. With Graham Stevens she has recently published *Managing Information for Research.*

Alan Poulter is a lecturer at the Department of Information and Library Studies at Loughborough University. He was previously a senior lecturer at Leeds Polytechnic having worked in the Science Museum Library and the British Library. He is also researching World Wide Web applications in libraries and Internet training.

Peter Gillman is one of the founding partners of The Information Partnership. Previously with the Aslib consultancy group and in various jobs with IBM.

Patricia Stoat spent fifteen years in the City before becoming Information Manager at Tyne and Wear Chamber of Commerce. She is now an information consultant working with the DTI on developing enquiry and information services for smaller businesses through Business Links.

David Smith is a Principal Librarian at the Department of Health responsible for implementing its Document and Information Management Strategy. He formerly worked for the European Parliament and Department of the Environment before being appointed Department of Health Systems Librarian in 1989.

Information for Tomorrow's Organisations

Introduction: Liz MacLachlan

Department of Trade & Industry

Two years ago the *Circle of State Librarians* conference looked at market testing and its impact on government library and information services.[1] Since then the shape of the Civil Service has changed significantly. The Fundamental Expenditure Review programme has redefined the role of many departments, removing some functions altogether and leading typically to reductions of around 20% in staffing. Senior Management Reviews, proposed in the Oughton report[2] and the white paper *Continuity and Change*[3], have now reported. Their aim is to produce a flatter organisation with fewer layers at the senior levels to manage the new departments. Emphasis is placed on giving individuals authority to do their jobs, with almost all departments working towards the *Investors in People* award.

Last year we identified some of the "levers for change" for the future of government library and information services, in particular open government and the INTERNET.[4] Developments over the past year, with many government departments setting up home pages, show how right we were. The government has (at last some might say) begun to wake up to the importance of electronic forms of communication in the world today. During 1995 CCTA held two high profile conferences on the Information Superhighway and has set up a number of COGS (Collaborative Open Groups) to continue discussion on the best way of promoting future development. In February the G7 group of countries agreed a number of research projects including one called Government On-Line whose purpose is to increase the amount of electronic communication between citizen and government. The goal is 50% of government business to be conducted electronically by the year 2000. So, by the end of the century in 5 years time, perhaps we will be able to file our self-assessment income tax forms, claim our social security benefits and register our vote in a referendum on devolution for Scotland, Wales and the English regions—electronically.

So the world is changing fast, both internally and externally. Where does this leave libraries? Our theme for the 1995 conference *Virtual libraries* is the role of libraries in tomorrow's organisation. Paradoxically perhaps, I believe that the changes in our environment place a greater than ever emphasis on good information. The impact of the changes we are seeing is to slim down and speed up the decision making process, fewer people will be taken more critical decisions in a faster timescale. If these decisions are to be good ones they need to be based on good information. Information services can play a key role in decision support. The information we supply will need to be high quality. That means

- *complete enough*: By inclination libraries are perfectionists, but in tomorrow's world it may take too long and be too expensive to produce a perfect, complete answer. Quality information is that which is "fit for purpose", it should tell the user what he needs, not everything known on the subject.

- *timely*: Both in terms of the information itself and our delivery of it. Rarely do our customers need the sort of real-time information used in the financial markets but they do need to know the latest state of play. I see greater emphasis on news sources and the networks for up-to-date information. And our customers need *some* information by their deadline not *all* of it three days late.

- *of known accuracy*: Our customers need know how far they can rely on the information supplied. Of course we want the information to be 100% right, but that takes time. Some sources are "better" than others. The hot news is on the Web, but commercial databases validate their information. We need to evaluate the sources and to take responsibility for what is found, perhaps even giving our customers a reliability rating.
- *useful*: Information needs to be presented to the user in a form he can digest and use immediately. With the tools we now have we can download from different sources, select, incorporate and repackage the answer—perhaps into a table or a graphic or a recommendation—then e-mail it directly to the user.

The challenge for us as managers is to refocus our information services and train our staff so that they can deliver information of this quality.

In the following papers Ray Lester outlines what is and what will happen to libraries in the very near future. He argues that libraries must add value for the organisation—or someone else will. Elizabeth Orna discusses how organisations use information and how, from her long experience of researching just this topic, they often fail to capitalise on what they have. Alan Poulter describes his research into visualisation techniques for information retrieval—translating the "big red book on the top of the shelf" into the personal library with all the key passages of the key texts arranged as the user wants them. Understanding user needs are essential to successful delivery of information, but oh so elusive. In his presentation Peter Gillman provides some clues on how to establish real user needs, and how information audits can help. Patricia Stoat, well known as an information professional herself, dons the guise of the elusive user. The points she makes about understanding the why as well as the what in a user's question and the crucial importance of training in sources may not be comfortable, but provide feedback essential to taking the service forward. Finally David Smith, from the Department of Health, shows what can be done with simple tools to deliver intelligence over the network.

References

1. Proceedings of the 1993 conference of the Circle of State Librarians, published as *Market testing and after*, edited by Lewis Foreman. London: HMSO, 1994.
2. Cabinet Office, Office of Public Service and Science, Efficiency Unit. *Career Management and Succession Planning Study*. (Oughton report). London: HMSO, 1993.
3. *The Civil Service: continuity and change*. (Cm 2627) London: HMSO, 1994.
4. Proceedings of the 1994 conference of the Circle of State Librarians, published as *Who needs libraries?*, edited by Lewis Foreman. London: HMSO, 1995.

The Role of the library in Tomorrow's Organisation

Ray Lester
Natural History Museum

My role in this opening address is to outline a number of key themes which might be considered in more detail in the succeeding papers at this Annual Study Conference. These themes may be conspiring—I will argue, *are* conspiring—to transform our present "real" libraries into "virtual" libraries. Given the many false dawns of the "paperless society" over the last two to three decades, it is easy this time around to discount what is happening: to assume that our predominantly paper-based libraries will continue in being much as they always have done over the last two to three centuries. But—as I have argued elsewhere[(1)]—believe you me: *this time IT is for real!*

All the building blocks are in place to create an infrastructure which will allow knowledge workers in industry, commerce, academia—*and* government and the public sector more generally—to acquire the published information and documents they need: not from your or my local departmental or institutional library; but from a remote virtual library store. The knowledge workers will do this—indeed, are already doing this—by electronically networking to the remote stores. Our libraries then must either change their roles; or they must die. We and our library staff colleagues who at present spend most or virtually all of our working lives facilitating the acquisition for stock of paper-based (and electronic: eg on CD-ROM) published material in anticipation of customer demand—*just-in-case*, must in future spend our working time facilitating the acquisition of published information and documents when customer demand for such material actually materialises: *just-in-time*.

In fact, even that, one could argue, will prove in the future to have been optimistic. Many of our present library customers already have on their desktops the same technological means to retrieve the information and documents they need, as the means we would use if we did the retrieval for, or with them. As time goes by, is it not becoming easier and easier to retrieve electronically from a remote location the published information and documents one needs via one or another "net"? With many such user-friendly systems coming on stream, all operating within an increasingly standardised workstation and local area networking environment (I think that it is called "Microsoft"!), surely anyone will soon be able to "surf the net" and get what published information and documents he or she needs. Schoolchildren do it all the time. No longer will we need librarians, information scientists or other information professionals to act as priestly gatekeepers at the portals of the world's cornucopia of public knowledge. Just as the staff intensive bank, the stockmarket trading floor, the corner shop, and so on, disappear under the onslaught of information technological advances, so will the library. The information superhighway beckons! The title of this Paper is "The role of the library in tomorrow's organisation". The answer: zilch! Don't waste your time staying around here listening to speaker after speaker intoning varients of the same litany. Leave now whilst there is still time. Get on your bike, and look for another job—Now!

That is the official version. That is what government in a cost saving mood would have us believe. Unfortunately—or, perhaps for this audience, fortunately—it is not that simple. For not only would I submit that "This time IT is for real", and thus we all have to respond to the IT imperative, to act. Also, I would suggest, "IT is complex". And so what I will try to do in the next half hour or so, is to remind each of you of some of that complexity. These glimpses of complexity—for that is all that is possible in an introductory overview of this type—are not meant to engender a despairing "Oh my God!: this is just too complicated, let's go and have a drink!". It is, I trust, an attempt to encourage an informed—shall we say, a *statesmanlike*—debate of the issues surrounding the notion of "virtual libraries"—amongst "real" librarians like you and me.

As in so many fields, the published articles and books and reports which one might read to get a grip on this complex domain, fall for the most part into two groups. There is the highly technical material, where academics (usually) engage in high-flown debate about the detailed nuances of the subject. Then there are the polemical articles written by busy practitioners who do not normally have the time to relate what they feel in their working bones to the more rigorous material available in the scholarly literature. I have tried to steer a middle course here: not shirking from alluding to items of difficulty (and there are many of those); but leaving the listener to follow one or another up later in the Papers which follow. Researchers and practitioners—not just in academia, where most of the high-flown debate has occurred so far, do need all to work effectively together to compose and sing the same song, if our libraries are not to be swept unthinkingly over the cliff edge into some sort of virtual abyss by those who currently finance them!

So: what are the sorts of difficulties with which we deal as we seek to make progress in defining a future role for our public sector libraries? Note that we *are* concerned with the *public sector* here: even though a lot of what has gone on in the last decade or so as regards the creation of agencies, market testing, and so on has blurred our old distinction between "public" and "private". Most, if not all of you here, for at least some of your operations, are directly or indirectly charged in some way by society (by parliament, by government), with providing customer access to a certain corpus, whether or not as librarians you would have chosen to if you had had a completely free hand in the matter. The fact that nowadays you are often required to charge those customers for access to the corpus you are charged with offering to those customers, merely further complicates an already difficult "public good" role.

What is a library? Here is a definition quoted in Sheila Corrall's booklet *Strategic Planning for Library and Information Services*(2). The definition is the "key purpose statement" of the *Information and Library Services Lead Body* (the UK development body for standards and vocational qualifications in information and library services—a part of the NVQ framework):

> "To determine/anticipate, stimulate and satisfy the information needs of existing and potential users/clients through the design and operation of systems for creating, synthesising, gathering,

categorising, storing, providing access to, retrieving, interpreting, and presenting information from all media and personal sources, in a cost effective manner, and by so doing, speeding the free flow of information to improve the business and social environment of an open society."

I will take six themes in turn from that definition:

- First, what I prefer personally as regards my own library operation, to term *customers*: we "customize" our library services for them. (They are called in the definition "users/clients".) We need "real" libraries because our customers need them. Once those customers stop needing them, we can close them all down.

- Second, what is perhaps implicit in the definition—by use of the phrase "all media"—the influence of *information technology* on the overall system with which we are concerned.

- Third, the notion of *publicly available information*. The definition actually encompasses both public and private information: but I will restrict us here to published information, because that is where the particularly difficult questions arise. (Actually, the really difficult questions are at the interface between public and private information: no doubt those will be dealt with in the next paper.)

- Fourth, the need to review future options within an *economic* framework—using that word as a catch-all to encompass such facets as cost/effectiveness.

- Fifth, a recognition that all libraries must be responsive to the *organizational mission and goals* of their parent organisation: certainly if their mandate includes "speeding the free flow of information to improve the business and social environment of an open society": what a large number of provocative implications there are in that phrase!

- Finally, sixth, the sub-system with which we are primarily concerned here: the libraries themselves—for which I prefer to use the more proactive designation *Information Centres*. As regards the role of such Centres encapsulated in this definition, I would particularly draw your attention to the words "synthesising" and especially "interpreting". The extent to which librarians in the future choose and are able to fulfill such value-adding roles will be a most significant determinant of their ability to survive in a virtual library environment. We will come back to value-adding , later.

Libraries—or *information centres*—then, are intermediary operations between those who produce *publicly available information* (authors and their publishers), and those who need to use such information, the *customers* of the library. The hypothesis is that those customers will increasingly bypass the library and get the published information they need without the intermediation of their local library and its staff, from some sort of virtual library. Advances in *information technology* seem the prime driver here: though it is interesting to reflect on the extent to which the *economics* of the whole system have become fundamentally more problematic in recent years because technology has enabled more information to be published in more forms and formats than it used to be, as well as raising the capabilities and expectations of customers to get at all this information. Or is the economic imperative itself actually the prime driver?: for example, less public money available for libraries than formerly, even though they must cope with both print and electronic resources, until the virtual library takes a real hold; an increasing commercialization amongst the publishers. Whatever the balance, a critical determinant of what happens in the future will be the explicit or implicit *organizational mission and goals* of the organization wherein lies the library: such as any "public good" roles of the type alluded to a moment ago. Obviously all of what happens must conform with the basic underlying *economics* of the overall system.

Before I say a little by example about each of these five parameters which comprise the basics of the system within which public sector libraries and information centres reside, let me summarise what I believe to be the key influences in each area:

"State Library **customers**, responsive—as ever—to *Zipf's Principle of Least Effort*, will increasingly via their parent organization's **information technology** *network infrastructure*, choose to retrieve the **publicly available information** they need in *real-time*, the relative **economics** of this primarily determined by the *intellectual property* laws applicable at the time to each needed chunk of information, the whole subject to any agreed *public good* responsibility resulting from the **organizational mission and goals**: and thus the customers will only continue to support the

> **information centres** with which they have traditionally used to the extent that the centres perform a *value-adding* function, over and above that provided by the internal/external network infrastructure the customers have direct access to."

Turning now to each of the system's six components in turn: what are the sorts of factor which will influence the role we might carve out in the future for our libraries?

The key phrase which I have suggested in the **customers** arena is *Zipf's Principle of Least Effort*. Zipf's Principle suggests that an overriding consideration for most of us is reducing effort. Even though in an academic context we **know** that a copy of the article that we need is available in the university library half a mile across campus, we will waste time searching our room for the copy we think that we stored somewhere in our filing cabinet a couple of years ago, because at the outset of the retrieval process, that seems as though it will involve less effort. Our customers increasingly have on their desks machinery which **seems** to offer the prospect of relatively effortless retrieval of publicly available information: at least, when compared to the effort of using our print-on-paper libraries. Other important characteristics of our present or potential library customers are:

- The key decision makers amongst our customer segments—the opinion formers—are exceptionally busy. These, critically, are also opinion formers in deciding the level of library resource allocation from the parent organization. We have to marshal our case very cogently.

- People networking is very important to all of our customers: such informal communication overwhelms the importance of the formal communication system of our customers.

- Otherwise, our customers for the most part keep up-to-date with developments through personally acquired newsletters, magazines, etc. and not via our libraries.

- Thus our libraries' roles in satisfying retrospective needs are more crucial than for satisfying current awareness needs.

- Customers are more and more happy to acquire information electonically: but generally they like to read anything substantial on paper.

- Our library customers are very reluctant to pay directly for information: that could prove very critical.

- Finally, intensive use of IT is increasingly a normal part of customer—civil servant—life.

Overall, as a gross generalisation, we might say that provided that the process is relatively effortless, and free of charge at the point of use, our present library customers will be more than happy in the future to retrieve the (retrospective) information and documents they need via their desktop workstations: rather than do this via your or my local library.

Note that this is not to say that our customers will henceforth cease to use print-on-paper as a convenient means of private perusal and storage of the publicly available information which they need to use. Nor that the transport of "published information" will be necessarily in the future a wholly electronic process. Substantial documents, especially those whose subject matter benefits from a sophisticated physical appearance, will still naturally be produced and bound as print-on-paper artefacts. Printed newspapers, newsletters and magazines will be purchased by individuals and groups and browsed through as now as a means of keeping broadly up-to-date with what is going on. But on the relatively rare occasions when *specific* (historical) data, information, or documents are needed and are not already in one's personal or workgroup "library", they will be identified and requested online: then to be speedily delivered to the "office" by courier, when online delivery of a digital version is not possible or acceptable.

In fact, the online delivery to the knowledge worker's desk of virtually any type of digital published compilation will very shortly become the norm. All that will hold up whether this is the transport route actually taken (apart from economic and legal considerations) will be the knowledge worker's ability locally to print the delivered compilation to the quality at that time required. The key phrase here then is *network infrastructure*. That infrastructure is now able, or will shortly be able, to carry all forms of:

- Data/text/image/moving image/voice/multimedia

Commercial pressures have boiled down the choice of desktop and server operating system environment to a very few candidates:

- Desktop: Apple—OS/2—Unix—Windows 95
- Server: Windows NT—Netware—Unix

High speed local area network backbones are being extended to the desktop. And the Internet continues to be a remarkable phenomenon linking together wide area networks of all sizes and shapes. The cost/performance for storage, processing and telecommunication of digitally encoded information and documents continues to improve dramatically, week on week.

The basic choice then becomes—for publicly available information—whether to locate it on a server within the local environment (eg on cd-rom); or whether to locate it externally. My personal feeling is that for the majority of publishing applications, the remote server solution will prove the winner—subject only and crucially to what happens in the intellectual property arena; and what is the pricing policy.

The virtual library will then—truly—be an electronic (and paper-based, but electronically addressable) library that does not exist within the organization: it only seems to exist there. Lest that seems fanciful, do not forget that our customers daily are accessing information, the electronic location of which, or the route via which they make electronic contact with the information, they neither know nor care. Our library customers are very used to switching between internally and externally created private information; they will become just as used to switching between internally and externally created shared public (or quasi-public) electronic information.

- *Access to internal private information* (The electronic office)
- *Access to extenal private information* (Electronic messaging)
- *Access to shared corporate information* (Database management)

- *Access to publicly available information* (The virtual library)

All this will happen in *real-time*. That is, the time-lag between what we might term the *generation* of information for the public domain:

- *Spoken* statement: eg press conference (almost invariably accompanied by a press release).
- *Electronic* statement: eg financial market data-feed; video feed.
- *Printed* statement: eg author's manuscript.

and what we might term its *display* within that domain:

- *Broadcast* radio, television;
- *Real-time electronic* the real-time data services;
- *Scheduled electronic* the traditional interactive online search services;
- *Print-on-paper* (and other portable physical artefacts: eg microform, CD-ROMS).

will shorten and shorten. Competitive pressures will ensure that: just as they have similarly where we need to keep up-to-date with what is happening via the more informal communication systems: we used to read newsletters; now more and more we read electronic bulletin boards or join list servers on the Internet.

Now, the system or systems for storing and transmitting all this publicly available electronic *data* translated by the system into meaningful statements we call *information*, to be then assimilated by our customer *knowledge* workers, who then use such knowledge to display, we trust, *wisdom*, all require a large capital investment.

That capital cost can either be financed by the *private sector* (publishers, electronic utilities, telecommunication companies etc.); or by the *public sector* (government under some guise, the British Library, public libraries, academic libraries, etc.); or by some combination of both groups. To take a simple example, the capital cost of acquiring and maintaining access to a database on cdrom held in one of your libraries is in the end being financed by the public purse; the capital cost for the same database stored on a remote private online host computer financed by the private sector database host. Traditionally—at least for textually based databases—the capital cost of the latter has been recouped by the host on a charge per use basis; but there is no reason why it could not be recouped as an annual subscription: such annual subscriptions with subsequent unlimited use are common with numerically based datasets (where, of course, there are normally no royalty complications). Traditionally also, libraries have often recouped from their customers the marginal cost of searching remotely stored databases; but they have not similarly recouped the capital cost of databases stored in-house (unless these, too, have a significant marginal cost of use).

I would suggest that in the future, if those who create and maintain the external virtual libraries which our customers will use themselves charge or continue to charge on a per use basis, the effect will be a move from a freely available internal information resource to a charged for external information resource. Not only that. As the internal library resource becomes relatively less and less important, will not organizations wish to move from supporting a freely available internal staff resource, to using only as needed an internal (or even, indeed, external) staff resource, whose capital cost is recouped on a charge per use basis. The latter sort of suggestion will be very familiar to many of you. Staff will no longer be needed on an ongoing basis to maintain the "real" library—because it no longer exists. They will be employed "just-in-time" rather than "just-in-case", and paid "just-in-time" rather than "just-in-case".

The economics of all this would be perfectly straightforward were it not for the peculiar characteristics of information as a resource, and the immense intellectual property complications which arise once one starts to deal with publicly available information, each of which in your case especially are aggravated further by your public good responsibilities.

On the last, public good, the difficulty in saying anything significant, is that one's statements very quickly become, or at least are interpreted as, political statements. But maybe in a Keynote Address given in the middle of the Party Conference season, it is allowable for one to indulge oneself somewhat. (Did I actually hear aright the other evening the current Leader of the Opposition use the words "library" and "free" very closely together in his speech to the Labour Party Annual Conference?) Maybe you—like me—have become concerned over the years at the erosion of the published print-on-paper corpus of official statistics: and thus its relative unavailability to large sectors of the national population. Maybe not. Maybe you have felt that there is a certain inconsistency in Parliament requiring companies to disclose financial and other material which might help those who would deal with the company assess its wholesomeness: yet at the same time making it relatively difficult for the man in the street to get at the resulting data. Maybe not. Maybe in this connection you have wondered why we can not in this country do what the Securities and Exchange Commission have done in the States: to make the basic data available as soon as is feasible, free of charge, on the Internet. Maybe not. Maybe you read with some concern of the privatisation of HMSO: does that body not exist to secure the full and uninhibited availability of information relevant to the workings of government. Perhaps I have misunderstood its prime role. And so on.

I have to say that to me, looking in from the outside, you seem to have a most difficult job. Working within a civil service framework, problematic enough at the best of times, you must—like any special library—balance out the allocation of inevitably limited resources amongst the different types of publicly available information and your different customer segments. On top of that , like me you are perhaps concerned at what government does or does not do with information. So, you try to do something about that to the extent to which you are allowed. Meanwhile, you must then try to make an effective response to the electronic imperative.

The beauty is that that imperative has the potential to solve the inequitable distribution of "government" information: as is, for instance, happening in the United States with the SEC, and elsewhere in government or quasi-government. Yet I suspect those of you who—like me—would wish to use the net to put to rights such inequity, are frequently being hampered by the seeming desire—of this present government—to make a business of information that by rights, belongs to the populace at large.

What is so exciting about the virtual library concept is that potentially it sweeps over the proverbial cliff into an abyss, all those in government who for "economic"reasons, would pussyfoot around with "our" information. No longer can it be argued that the country cannot "afford" to provide copies of "official" and "quasi-official" information in all the locations where cost/beneficial use would be made of them: the information is simply put up on the Web (or whatever will replace that protocol). Then, librarians—such as you and me—can concentrate on our real role of adding value for our customers to the electronic (and non-electronic) information publicly available worldwide.

What, then, is the future role for librarians?

- Support the organizational strategy: despite perhaps your (and my) disagreements with many elements of our parent organization's strategy, in the end we must work in tandem.
- Help engineer the infrastructure: this must be there: it must be fast and sophisticated, and do what librarians need: not what computer people think that we and our customers need.
- Merge with cognate services: and if you cannot get the computer people to do what is needed, take them over!
- Provide customer training and education: this is our fundamental role for the future. Do not, for God's sake, try to stop the move to self-service. Help the customers achieve this: then concentrate on the things that they cannot: such as defining the internal data architecture.
- Define our professionalism: we must work more on what uniquely we can contribute.
- Value-add: otherwise, someone else will.

Reference

Lester, R: 'This time IT is for real!' *Law Librarian 25*, 1994, pp 181–5.

How Organisations use information

Elizabeth Orna
Orna Stevens Associates

This paper takes as its starting point a quotation from the Conference programme: "*every day there are new ways for people to get at the information they need to do their jobs. But what information is that?*"

It looks at the evidence for:

- What organisations think is the information they need in order to achieve their objectives;
- How that affects their ideas and actions about the information that the people who work in them need in order to do their jobs.

It then considers what they *really* need to know to stay in business and prosper, and what that implies for their use of information and for the development of an "information culture". Finally, it offers some ideas about the role that information managers can claim in moving their organisations towards a productive use of information and the technologies which allow so many new ways of access.

Some initial definitions. It seems only fair at the outset to give readers an indication of how I define the terms to which I refer throughout this paper.

Organisations. This definition is designed to be applicable to any kind of organisation, from social club to government department, from manufacturing firm to service businesses; from pressure group to educational institution. Organisations are: groupings of people into "socio-technical systems" (Eason, 1988)[1], for explicit or implicit purposes, which include creating "offerings" of products, services, or combinations of the two. They interact both internally and with their environment; they seek "sustenance" to keep in being; and they have a structure and a boundary.

If those features are "singly necessary and jointly sufficient" for being an organisation, we can define the kinds of knowledge and know-how organisations need on order to survive as:

- What is happening inside its boundaries;
- What is happening in its "outside world", in the other systems which impinge on it;
- How to recognise, interpret and act on significant changes, within and without;
- How to create appropriate products/services;
- How to communicate.

I make no claims for originality in the definitions of knowledge and information which follow; they go back to ideas elegantly expressed by Brookes (1980)[2] and more recently by such theorists as Ingwersen (1992)[3].

Knowledge. What we acquire from our interaction with the world; the results of experience stored inside our minds, which we use to guide our actions. It comes in two main forms: knowledge *about* things and *know-how.* We make it our own by *transforming* the information that comes from outside into internal knowledge.

Information. Knowledge made visible or audible and put into the world in the form of "information products". What we transform our knowledge into when we want to communicate it to others. We can also usefully think of it as the *food of knowledge*, because we need information and communication to nourish and maintain our knowledge and keep it in good shape for what we need to do. Without constant nourishment with appropriate information, knowledge belonging to individuals and to organisations depreciates and can lead them into trouble.

It follows form this definition that individuals and organisations have to make their own definitions of what constitutes information—what is vital for one, can be interesting but irrelevant or totally incomprehensible for another. This is so obvious that it is almost embarrassing to mention it, but readers may like to ask themselves how many organisations they know which have actually defined what constitutes information for their purposes.†

And while information is sometimes now described as "the fourth resource", it has some peculiarities not shared with other material resources:

- To have value, it has to be transformed by human cognitive processes into human knowledge, without which no products of tangible value can be produced or exchanged. Its value lies in its use.
- If hoarded, it can actually fail to achieve its full potential value for those who hoard it, but if it is exchanged and traded, the value resulting from use increases for all parties to the transaction (collaboration is not the antithesis of competition!)
- It is a diffused resource, entering into all activities of organisations and forming a component of all their products and services.
- And, not only is it diffuse, it is also compressible and extendable; it can be shared or consumed more than once; it is long-lasting and does not necessarily decrease with use; and it can substitute for other resources such as labour or capital.

What do organisations think they need to know in order to meet their objectives? There is a question that ought, perhaps, to precede that one: "What do organisations think their objectives mean?"

---

†There is perhaps some encouragement to be found in the initiative of the Hawley Committee (1995)[(4)] under the KPMG IMPACT programme, which proposes that 'all significant information in an organisation, regardless of its purpose, should be properly identified. . . for consideration as an asset of the business' (though some aspects of its checklist suggest that the Committee has not given itself the benefit of consulting professionals in information management!)

". . . while there are few enterprises without some kind of statement of what they are in business for, a detailed look at what is on paper, combined with an analysis of what key people say about the matter, can reveal that the statement of objectives is either:

- Out of date in relation to the current environment
- Irrelevant to the enterprise's present directions
- Unknown to people who work for the enterprise
- Disregarded
- Interpreted in different ways in different parts of the enterprise"

(Orna, 1990)[5]

It seems, indeed, that the meaning of objectives is not usually considered a subject for polite conversation in organisations. Hepworth's (1992)[6] research on involving users of information in the health service in system design showed that the participants found this a "rare opportunity, as a group of professionals within their units, to discuss together the objectives of their work and the information implications of those objectives." Variations in perceptions emerged, leading to the conclusion that "Whatever [system] design process is adopted should elicit from the potential users of the system such variations which might exist in their perceptions of role and objectives."

Within my own experience there is the case of an organisation which had carried out an information audit without first trying to derive information requirements from corporate objectives. There were then difficulties in making sense of the audit findings for presentation to management, and a consultant had to be asked to do retrospectively what should have been done at the beginning, so that there was something against which the audit findings could be matched.

If organisations do not pay much attention to getting an agreed interpretation of their objectives, they are not particularly well placed for deciding what knowledge they need in order to achieve them, or what information they require to feed their knowledge.

The fundamental failure to make a specific organisational definition of information, or even to realise that it is possible or necessary to do so, probably underlies other shortcomings attested by research. Organisations tend to lack an overview of what information is held, where it is, who has it, and what they do with it. Davenport (1993)[7] makes the point that "much information in organizations and processes—more than 85%, by some estimates—is not manipulated by information technology". More significance is accorded to the quantitative than the qualitative, to the highly structured than the less structured, to the internally originating rather than information from the outside world. To quote Davenport again, the result is that "despite much talk and writing about the 'Information Age' few organizations have treated information management as a domain worthy of serious improvement efforts. Progress in managing information is rarely described or measured; providers of less-structured information in organizations (eg libraries, competitive analysis functions, and market research groups) often have relatively low status and confused reporting relationships; vast amounts of information enter and leave organizations without anyone's being fully aware of their impact, value, or cost."[8]

Again, particularly in the matter of information perceived as "strategic" (a perception likely to be unreliable for reasons discussed above), content is less highly regarded than the technologies used to gain access to it, and information is not considered of strategic importance unless it is handled via the latest technology. This may account for Galliers' report (1993)[9], that senior managers see information systems strategy as a critical issue, but one full of problems, which include the difficulty in integrating IS strategy with business strategy, differing views of key stakeholders about what information systems strategy is supposed to achieve, and difficulties in measuring benefits. In reality, IT of itself cannot provide a company with competitive advantage: "IT is every company's solution. The advantage instead goes to those organizations that develop a sound strategy, grounded in well-formulated business practices, and that execute it effectively. In this context, IT may be the enabler of the strategy."[10]

Drucker (1995)[11] assesses the situation succinctly; he considers that since data processing tools first appeared 30–40 years ago, business people have both over- and under-rated the importance of information in the organization. They have assigned great significance to the new tools for handling and delivering information, but have failed to realise how they would change tasks and enable them to see businesses differently—as creatures/creators of the material environment—that "area outside the organization in which opportunities and results lie, but in which the threats to the success and the survival of every business also originate."

He also makes a significant point which is not yet widely appreciated by organisations which aspire to become knowledge-based: investing in IT for the purpose will not reduce the costs of human resources: "in knowledge-based work especially, additional capital investment will likely require more, rather than less, labour".[(12)]

The information that people need in order to do their jobs. Given that organisations on the whole do not make a brilliant showing in defining what information they need to achieve their objectives, or what they need to do with it, how do they manage when it comes to providing the people who work for them with the information they require to do their jobs? Observation suggests the ideas are pretty limited, and the actions to implement them are often more so. Organisational structures—especially those in which individual departments or constituent businesses enjoy near-autonomy—often mean fragmented decision making about information needs, and impose near-impermeable barriers to interchanges of information which is essential for effective work by people on either side of the barriers. "Businesses inhibit the flow of information; they keep individuals and groups isolated and reinforce preconceptions." (Garvin, 1993)[(13)]

Decisions about what information people need to do their jobs are often taken at a point remote from those who do the work, by managers who have no notion of how the jobs are actually done but who presume to decide on job-holders' behalf what is essential and what is just "nice to know". There is seldom a serious and consistent effort to allow job-holders to define what they actually need in their work. Nor are there organisational "meeting places" where different work groups can tell each other what they need from each other. Yet, when the opportunity is given for people to explain what they need from colleagues and why they need it, it is usually not too difficult to negotiate solutions, and the benefits are immediate and cheaply achieved.

Even in organisations which have committed themselves to "open communication" more emphasis is still placed on top-down flow of information, than on the opposite direction, and lateral flows can still be seen as subversive in "federal" type organisations. Typically, there is top-down internal communication of information about what the organisation is up to: via meetings where managers pass on information from briefing meetings higher up the chain, internal newsletters, circulars, procedural instructions, employee handbooks etc. At the top end, managers are served by management information systems or executive information systems which—again because information is narrowly defined—do not give access to a full range of externally originating information, and provide internally originating information which is less than optimal. (As Davenport, 1993, puts it, "most firms concentrate on financial information generated from accounting systems, which, as has been widely recognized, is frequently misleading or useless for management purposes"[(14)]). Holohan, 1992, reporting on research about whether performance indicators on executive information systems helped towards achieving strategic objectives, observes that "unfortunately, not one organisation which took part in the research modelled its EIS in its overall business strategy, thus limiting the use of their EIS to that of a glorified fire extinguisher rather than using it to help bridge the gap between formulating and implementing a business strategy."[(15)]

Other unproductive barriers exist between the processes of communicating information inside and of communicating information from the organisation to the outside world. The result is that people inside the organisation do not know about, for example, the information products that go to the customers or clients with whom they deal in the course of their work. And the resources of information in libraries and information services all too often remain unknown and ignored by those who make decisions on the organisation's information products, as they are organisationally and culturally separated from other information sources and systems. Typically, the process of getting information to people is split up among a number of different departments, with differing status and few formal links, for example Communications Department, Press and Public Relations, Personnel, Corporate Services, Information Systems, etc.

And the technology in use often undermines rather than supports what people need to do with information. Staff do daily battle with systems that make it either impossible or very difficult to get information of the kind and in the form they need. In the course of my own research over the past year, I have encountered membership databases which make it impossible to find information about members which could be used to design new information products; museum information systems which cannot be interrogated directly by curators, but require specialist help; and customer databases which cannot be used to assemble indicators which would help decisions about new, tailored products.

At the same time, the technology which is available in organisations is not used adequately in creating the day-to-day information products which people need to consult in their work. They are often badly designed, low-grade documents which make it hard to find and use the relevant information. If organisations forget—as they often appear to—that information has value only when a human mind has transformed it into knowledge and applied it to do something useful, then they are unlikely to realise the loss of value that comes from giving it to people in ways that make it hard to transform and use.

What do organisations really need to know? What information do they need to feed their knowledge? What do they need to do with it? It may be useful here to remind readers of the definition of the knowledge which organisations need, as a preliminary to citing some research findings:

- What is happening inside its boundaries;
- What is happening in its 'outside world', in the other systems which impinge on it?
- How to recognise, interpret and act on significant changes, within and without;
- How to create appropriate products/services;
- How to communicate.

Drucker's recent (1995) paper, quoted earlier, summarises the needs for information about the outside world like this:

"For *strategy* we need organised information about the environment—information about markets, customers, and non-customers; about technology in one's own industry, and others, about world-wide finance; and about the changing world economy".[16] Companies are, however, bad at using available information of this kind. "Many US companies went into Europe in the 1960s without even asking about labor legislation."

Davenport (1993)[17] outlines the roles that information about themselves and their relationships, could, with benefit to organisations, play in the whole range of business processes, including the creation of appropriate products:

- Performance monitoring;
- Process integration—information is the "glue" that holds an organisational structure together;

- Management of customer information to allow tailoring of products and services;
- Information-oriented management processes that make use of unstructured and externally generated information, in ways that combine human analytical skills with sophisticated technology.

The literature of research on innovation (usefully summarised by Bowden and Ricketts, 1992)[18] provides many pointers towards how organisations should bring together information from inside and the environment in order to recognise, interpret and act on change. Risk in innovation is minimised by being able to draw on full resources of internal information and good communication between upstream and downstream operations. Success is supported teams from different functions working together, good communications inside firms and between them and their outside world, clear lines of communication and free sharing of information, and informal information structures.

And so far as competition is concerned, the research findings about the use of information may be rather unexpected for many organisations. Success in competition depends on having and understanding information about competitors, collaborators and suppliers; information exchange and good lines of communication between professionals from the same discipline who are employed in different businesses; and knowing what information should be kept within the organisation and what can with benefit be shared—"What one keeps to oneself and what one shares is . . . the essence of management of competition" (Bower, 1992)[19]. The research evidence (eg Bowonder and Miyake, 1992)[20] also suggests that wide environmental monitoring and organisational learning, rather than simply investing in advanced IT, is the basis for sustained competitive advantage.

Norman and Ramirez (1993) define the assets that really matter in "an economy founded on the new logic of value" as knowledge and relationships with people on the receiving end of the organisation's "offerings", and they have to be integrated so that there is "a better and better fit between relationships and and knowledge"[21]. The organisation ". . . must invest in an ever-broadening range of knowledge resources and combine ever-expanding kinds of knowledge into its offerings".[22]

The implications of all this for the use of information by organisations can be summarised in Garvin's words (1993)—they need to become "skilled at creating, acquiring and transferring knowledge, and at modifying [their] behaviour to reflect new knowledge and insights."[23] In other words, they need to become *learning organisations*. By definition, a learning organisation is one that appreciates and uses to the full skills in managing information, in every aspect of its use of information, especially in managing unstructured information and information from its outside world in ways that in Davenport's words "combine human analytical skills with sophisticated technology".[24] To summarise, organisations need to:

- Define information in their own terms, in relation to their key objectives;
- Identify the people who need to use it, and how they need to use it;
- Build up a comprehensive picture of what information they have, and what they are doing with it;
- Identify gaps between what they need and what they have, between what they are doing with it and what they should be doing;
- Know about their "customers" and their outside world, and integrate that knowledge with self-knowledge, in order to deliver the value-added products and services which will enable them to achieve their objectives;
- Promote internal information flow, and the interchange of information with their "outside world";
- Integrate information technology to support users in doing the things *they* need to do with information;
- Monitor developments in the technology and select for investment technology which gives the potential for further constructive use of information.

An information culture. If organisations were to develop their thinking about information and its use in these ways, the people who work for them would benefit from an "information culture". Information would be better understood, probably less talked about, and its full use would become an integral part of work. The distinguishing characteristics of an information culture:

- Enriched understanding of what information is;
- Use of information as seen as an ordinary regular part of everybody's job, not as the province of specialists, nor yet as an optional extra or something only done on special occasions;
- Close and organic relation between information and decision making—not something sought at the last moment to buttress decisions already taken, or provided but ignored, but constantly absorbed and used at all stages;
- Imaginative rather than conventional use of IT;
- Internal information politics the subject of open negotiation; acknowledgment of the legitimate areas of interest of stakeholders;
- Understanding of other people's needs for information, and of who needs to be told what in order to do their own job;
- Information flowing laterally as well as vertically and management recognition of the importance of lateral flow;
- Ability to respond organically, as an "intelligent community" to external threats, rather than in a fragmented self-destructive way;
- Sharper awareness of change and better anticipation to take advantage of it rather than make the worst of it.

What roles can information professionals prepare to claim?

The purpose of this Conference is to "address the way that networks and user-friendly systems are making information more accessible to users outside the traditional library". That formulation suggests some perception of a threat to organisational libraries and information services, but I would prefer to think of current changes as an opportunity to take advantage of. Why not use the greater accessibility of information to individuals via technology as a means of setting the agenda and taking a lead in redefining the role of information and its management? Who, after all, has a better right or is better equipped than informational professionals to lead in information culture?

With that in mind, here are some initiatives that seem worth considering:

- Study how people in the organisation actually make individual use of electronic sources; find people with expertise; note where they have difficulty in using the sources; identify the kinds of job-related knowledge which are not available from individual access to electronic sources. (And it should be remembered that, even if individuals can find a lot of information for themselves, they are not likely to be particularly adept at managing and retrieving it!)
- Use the process of finding answers to those questions as a means of interaction with potential clientele; it could form a starter or an element for an information audit, and become the basis for policy development.
- Present recommendations to management on what individuals can usefully do for themselves, on what the organisation's information services can provide which is not accessible in any other way, on how the service should develop to complement what people are getting for themselves, and on developing a technology monitoring programme.*
- Establish a lead role as the knowledge base for all the organisation's information resources—knowing what resources are where, and promoting their integrated use.
- Aim to become the centre for knowledge about organisational learning, and about valuation of information resources.

The Drucker paper quoted earlier has some interesting suggestions, too: "The majority of enterprises have yet to start the job" of building systems to gather and organise outside information. To do it, they need specialised skills and knowledge: "What we need are services

* "To ensure that they always get the most out of IT, companies need a . . . team of technical experts to help them stay on top of changing technology, changing business needs, and the changing capabilities of . . . IT providers . . . Another of the team's primary responsibilities is to assess emerging technologies. New technologies . . . may sound very tempting, but will the company really be able to take advantage of them? The answer is no or not yet in a surprising number of instances" (Lacity *et al*, 1995)[(26)]

that make specific suggestions about how to use the information, ask specific questions regarding the users' business and practices, and perhaps provide interactive consultation" ". . . a new and radically different view of the meaning and purpose of information: as a measurement on which to base future action rather than as a post-mortem and a record of what has already happened."[(25)] The only odd thing about those proposals is that their author seems to believe that organisations need "outsiders" for developing this work. He seems to be unaware that what he is asking for is in fact within the competance of good information managers in many organisations!

References

1. Eason, K: *Information technology and organisational change.* Taylor & Francis, 1988.
2. Brookes, B C: "Informatics as the fundamental social science" *In* P Taylor, *ed: New Trends in documentation and information.* Proceedings of the 39th FID Congress. Aslib, 1980.
3. Ingwersen, P: "Information and information science in context" *Libri 42* (3) 1992 pp 99–135.
4. Hawley Committee: *Information as an asset.* A consultative document for chairmen, chief executives and boards of directors. KPMG IMPACT programme, 1995.
5. Orna, E: *Practical information policies.* Gower, 1990.
6. Hepworth, J B *et al*: "The enhancement of information systems through user involvement in systems design" *International Journal of Information Management 12*, 1992, p 128.
7. Davenport, T H: *Process innovation—Re-engineering work through information Technology.* Boston, Mass, Harvard Business School Press, 1993, p 71.
8. *op cit*, p 72.
9. Galliers, R D: "IT strategies: beyond competitive advantage" *Journal of Strategic Information Systems 2* (4) 1993 pp 283–291.
10. *op cit*, p 28.
11. Drucker, P F: "The information executives truly need" *Harvard Business Review* January–February 1995 p 54.
12. *op cit*, p 59.
13. Garvin, D A: "The learning organisation" *Harvard Business Review* July–August 1993 p 91.
14. *op cit.*
15. Holohan, J: "The use of executive information systems in measuring business performance" *Journal of Information Technology 7* 1992 pp 177–186.

16. *op cit* p 61.
17. *op cit.*
18. Bowden, A *and* Ricketts, M *Eds*: *Stimulating innovation in industry: the challenge for the United Kingdom.* Kogan Page/NEDO, 1992.
19. Bower, J L: *The organisation of markets.* Harvard Business School, Division of Research, 1992. (Working Paper, 92-032).
20. Bowonder, B *and* Miyake, T: "Creating and sustaining competitiveness: information management strategies of Nippon Steel Corporation" *International Journal of Information Management 12* 1992 pp 39–56.
21. Norman R *and* Ramirez, R: From value chain to value constellation: designing interactive strategy. *Harvard Business Review 71* 1993 p 77.
22. *op cit*, p 74.
23. Garvin, D A: "The learning organisation." *Harvard Business Review* July–August 1993 pp 78–91.
24. *op cit.*
25. *op cit*, p 62.
26. Lacity, M D *et al*: "IT outsourcing: maximise flexibility and control" *Harvard Business Review* May–June 1995 pp 84–93.

Towards the Networked Virtual Reality Library

Alan Poulter

Department of Information and Library Studies, Loughborough University

The first task is to explain the title of this paper. A *virtual reality library* is a self-coined phrase which I defined as: " the bibliographic data from a typical library collection. . . being accessed via an interface which looks, on screen, like a roomful of shelves and which a user would navigate and control using a device like a 3D mouse"[1].

A virtual reality library then is a form of OPAC, which would work in the same way as the physical structure and contents of a library (rooms, shelves and books). Because it relies on a 3D image on a computer screen, some form of *virtual reality* software is required. Thus virtual reality library is a convenient short-hand way of referring to a new concept in OPAC design. It is distinct from the term *virtual library*, which refers to a collection of materials accessed via a telecommunications network.

The rationale for such an OPAC is that it works by allowing users to browse physical space for information, in much the same way as they would browse in a real library. Ever since libraries came into being browsing and shelf access have been important retrieval methods. Rather than have to frame queries, users would browse the virtual reality library. Browsing depends solely on a person's natural ability to recognize an ordering of items on shelves and it is this ordering which makes browsing a viable strategy. Because similar items are stored together, browsing involves looking for one relevant item, on the assumption that its neighbours might also be relevant. While shelf orders can be understood by common sense reasoning, working on the example of ordered items in sight, no such strategy exists for the current generation of OPACS. With them the onus is on the user to build up a conceptual model in their mind of how such an OPAC works. With a virtual reality library, there is no disjunction between conceptual model (the information space) and appearance (library-like display).

Virtual reality. It is appropriate at this point to consider the feasibility of using virtual reality technology, since the creation of a virtual reality library prototype requires its usage. The 1993 volume of the *Annual Review of Information Science and Technology* included for the first time a review of virtual reality technology, and a preliminary overview of its applications in information work[2]. Extremely cheap "desktop virtual reality" software packages, which can create just the sort of display required for a virtual reality library, are now available via the Internet[3].

One such, REND386, was used to build a prototype of a virtual reality library[4]. A rather basic display of a library structure was used to house a small number of bibliographic records. Access to items in shelf orders by title, author, subject and classification code was allowed. This prototype had many of the functions of the proposed full-version, but not all. For example, it was proposed that once a user had located a relevant item, its copies in other shelf orders would be highlighted, to encourage browsing in those locations for related items, which might also be relevant. REND386 was essentially a visualiser, in that it took in the description of a virtual world (known as a world database) and rendered (drew) that virtual world on a computer screen. The 3D effect is produced by the visualiser by drawing objects in a particular order, so that "far" objects are drawn before "near" objects, causing the latter to overwrite the former. A visualiser continually redraws the virtual world as the user changes position and viewpoint in that world, by interacting with it via a standard mouse or keyboard. The world database comes from a world file, and ancilliary object files, which are reusable if need be.

Objects are expressed in terms of polygons (flat straight-sided shapes) and their vertex coordinates. The biggest problem with using REND386 was the difficulty of rendering text in the virtual world.

The virtual reality library prototype built with REND386 demonstrated the workings of a virtual reality library. One could simply browse through a shelf ordering, following textual signs to representational graphics of bibliographic items. However it could not interface with bibliographic records on a CD, nor those in an OPAC. This would have required extra programming and possible reprocessing of the bibliographic data for suitable rendering. Potentially the most useful application of the virtual reality library prototype would have been to access a remote library collection,via a network. This would be a *networked virtual reality library.* This also was not possible using REND386.

Virtual Reality Modeling Language. It can be argued that the development of the Internet has had three distinct phases; first, the development of the TCP/IP infrastructure which allowed documents and data to be stored at named network repositories/sites. While this provision was useful, it was also confusing; without any clear sense of "what went where", and access to Internet was restricted to the class of "net surfers" who could maintain their own cognitive map of data locations. Remote access to standard library OPACS was possible. Hytelnet[5] provides a comprehensive listing.

The second phase began with Tim Berners-Lee's work at CERN, where he developed the hypermedia system known as World Wide Web. Web "pages" containing text and multimedia resources could be constructed using the Hypertext Markup Language (HTML), a derivative of the Standard Generalised Markup Language (SGML). Hypertext links between pages used an "addressing" scheme, a unique identifier (the Universal Resource Locator), which could tell anyone "where to go and how to get there" for any page on the Web. A number of pioneering libraries[6] have created Web interfaces for their OPACS. These allow local access via graphical Web browser software, and also remote access via the Internet. This arrangement works by passing searches input via a Web page to an intermediary software program which processes searches so that a traditional OPAC can handle them, and returns the results via a special Web page.

While being a major advance and leading to the Internet's current popularity, Web pages lack dimensionality; and the only type of navigation permissible is by hypertext. Pages on the Web can only be referred to by URLs such as http://foo.bar.com/docs/home.html, which has all the memorability of bibliographic citations

This is shortly to change, as a new standard, Virtual Reality Modeling Language (VRML), for viewing Web pages has appeared, which allows pages to be rendered as 3D images. This is going to usher in a third phase of the development of the Internet. VRML was conceived in the spring of 1994 at the first annual World Wide Web Conference in Geneva, Switzerland. Tim Berners-Lee and Dave Raggett organized a special session to discuss virtual reality interfaces to the World Wide Web. Attendees agreed on the need for a common language for specifying 3D scene description and Web hypertext links—an analog of HTML for virtual reality. The term Virtual Reality Markup Language (VRML) was coined, and the group resolved to begin specification work after the conference. The word "Markup" was later changed to "Modeling" to reflect the graphical nature of VRML.

The basis of VRML is a subset the Open Inventor ASCII File Format from Silicon Graphics, Inc. The inventor File Format supports complete descriptions of 3D scenes with polygonally rendered objects, lighting, materials, ambient properties and realism effects. Silicon Graphics has publicly stated that the file format is available for use in the open market, and have contributed a file format parser into the public domain to speed VRML viewer development.

The VRML specification (currently at 1.0) is platform independent, extensible, workable over low-bandwidth connections and supports hypertext links. At the most basic, VRML is just a way for 3D objects to display themselves. Objects are called "nodes". Nodes can be arranged in hierarchical structures called "scene graphs" which define an ordering for the rendering of the nodes, allowing the drawing of 3D scenes. A node had fields for the type of object (eg cube), display parameters (eg scaling) and an identifying name. An example VRML file containing a simple scene defining a view of a red cone and a blue sphere, lit by a directional light follows:

```
#VRML V1.0 ascii
Separator {
DirectonalLight {
direction 0 0 – 1 # Light shining from viewer into scene}
PerspectiveCamera {
position –8.6 2.1 5.6
```

```
orientation –0.1352 –0.9831 –0.1233 1.1417
focalDistance 10.84
}
Separator { # The red sphere
Material {
diffuseColor 1 0 0 # Red
}
Translation { translation 3 0 1 }
Sphere { radius 2.3 }
}
Separator { # The blue cube
Material{
diffuseColor 0 0 1 # Blue
}
Transform {
translation –2.4 .2 1
rotation 0 1 1 .9
}
Cube {}
}
```

Virtual Reality Markup Language has a potential application for building 3D interfaces to collections of information on the Internet. A prime-mover behind the development of VRML, Mark Pesce[8], proposed:—

> "Vision Two: The United States Library of Congress
> When: October 1994
> The Project:
> My initial inspiration for the creation of Labyrinth and VRML was to develop a way to model the complexity and richness of the Web in such a manner that it is intriNsically navigable, without any instruction required on anyone's part. I use, as an example, the US Library of Congress GOPHER site. It is rich, it is deep, but it is difficult to navigate or browse, especially if one is unaquainted with the site, or one doesn't know precisely what one is looking for.
> I assert that it is possible to model the Web in three dimensions in such a way that it is—intrinsically—navigable, such that the form of an object within a particular space is derived from the content of that object. It is possible, then, to build a "library", or data repository, which looks coincidentally like a library in the real world; in fact, we are better served if this virtual library looks like its

> content. If we succeed in this, it should be possible for anyone, of any age, to browse the collected content of the world's greatest library (or as much of it as they care to place on-line), without having to be taught hermetic classification systems, searching methodologies, and the like."

Conclusion. As Mark Pesce notes, rather than create HTML pages as interfaces to existing OPACS, it is now possible to use VRML. A growing range of VRML Web browsers and tools is available[7]. Work is now proceeding to use a convertor to turn REND386 virtual world files into VRML files. These can then be displayed by a VRML browser. A test database of bibliographic records is being put onto a Web server, and software to act as an intermediary between this database and VRML files is being written. A prototype of a truly networked virtual reality library is under construction.

References

1. Poulter, Alan: "Towards a virtual reality library". *Aslib Proceedings.* 1993, *45*(1), pp 11-17.
2. Newby, G B: "Virtual reality". *Annual Review of Information Science and Technology.* 1993, 28, pp 187-229.
3. VR software (from Chris Hand's VR page): URL:- http://www.cms.dmu.ac.uk/People/cph/vrsw.html.
4. Poulter, Alan: "Building a browsable virtual reality library". *Aslib Proceedings.* 1994,46(6), pp151-154.
5. Hytelnet. <URL:- http://moondog.usask.ca/hytelnet/>
6. Libweb. <URL:-http://www.lib.washington.edu/tdowling/libweb.html>
7. The VRML Repository. <URL:- http://www.sdsc.edu/vrml/>
8. Email message to : www-vrml@wired.com (vrml), subject: PHIL: VRML Visions, date: Sun, 12 Jun 1994 21:38:57 -0700 (PDT)

Clear Away Mirages and Spot Mutants: what information audits tell you about user needs

Peter Gillman

The Information Partnership

One of the few perceptible benefits of market testing as far as libraries in Government service were concerned, was the opportunity to specify in fine detail exactly what services were provided, to whom, with what resources, where, and when. Of course the specification process really required two goes: the first to try and establish what was happening; and the second to specify what should happen. We know from our work that for a number of senior managers to whom librarians reported, reading these specifications was often a wholly novel experience. For many of these managers it was the first time they had actually faced the richness of service provision, or the complexity of it.

The whole process of specification flushed out many spectres and skeletons that required decent burial. Agencies and quangos with historic (but no longer organisational) ties to their parent Departments were shown up as service users although there was no obvious way of getting any recompence for this activity. The extent of service provision had usually been hidden or "lost"; and the fact that it happened at all had often been beyond the authority of the

Librarian to control. So writing a specification, perhaps in the form of a matrix of service users *vs* the resources needed to support them, allowed those spectres to be examined in the light of day.

The roots of this situation lie in the fact that for many libraries in Government service, the authority to carry out long-term planning of service provision on terms of targeting support for critical user groups has been something that they have been denied. Services have therefore grown up in a totally *ad hoc* fashion. They have been driven by cost and not value, by budget and not benefit. Resources have been applied if they were available, but frequently with little or no chance to look at the needs of particular user groups and define optimum services for them.

Why did this happen and what, if anything, can be done about it? The "why" part is complex, based on a combination of ignorance of the information industry among senior managers, an inability to see that almost all jobs depend to some extent on a regular information flow, an unwillingness to see departmental operations in terms of an integrated whole but instead as discrete packets called branches, and the curse of the annual budget cycle.

The annual budget, where it does not build on what went before but starts afresh each time, is the crude tool of organisations driven by political whim and not business development. Resources, the provision of which may have taken a year to implement, and a year to build up to a reasonable performance level, are completely at the mercy of the bean counters.

My title came directly from a discussion we had in the office over lunch when trying to map out the contents of this paper. 'Clear away mirages' obviously means 'let's take a look at what is going on, and try to understand its origins and effects'. Mirages occur in deserts, where everywhere looks the same, and to make it worse they distort the view. Get them out of the way, and perhaps it is possible to see that there are some landmarks that are useful for navigation. 'Spot mutants' is a bit harder to explain. Not all mutants have green hair and three arms: often the mutation is not obvious at all. Mutants are services, or users, or resources, that are not quite what they seem. The completely inefficient service that is bomb-proof because it operates under the personal patronage of a senior person, is the sort of mutant that it can be quite hard to spot. The electronic source that is printed out for distribution because distribution has always been on paper, is a little easier to see.

Real user needs. The real needs of users, or the needs of real users? Is there a difference? Discuss (35 marks). Users have two kinds of need: the first is for what they *believe* they want; while the second is for what they actually require. Often the first completely swamps the second. This is because the services available tend to bias expectations. It is extraordinarily difficult to get people to say things like "I need good, rapid access to debates in the House". Instead they will tell you that they must see *Hansard*. Why? because they have lost sight of the debates, being able to see only the known means to deliver them. Libraries do this to people. Users ask for what they believe they are likely to get, but not what they actually want. They will ask for an atlas and not a street map, because they know you have one but think that you might not have anything so mundane as a street map. They will ask for a particular reference book instead of for the information that they want, which may come from it. It is the same process at work that makes someone ask for a dictionary when what they really want to know is the meaning of the word *taghairm*.

It is fair to say that librarians perpetuate the problem by often imagining or supposing what the needs of users are, without testing the supposition. This situation arises through information staff concentrating on the resources they have available, instead of what those resources contain. More of this later. The first trick of user needs studies is therefore to get behind the expressed needs to find the underlying ones.

The picture is something like this if you look at the user:

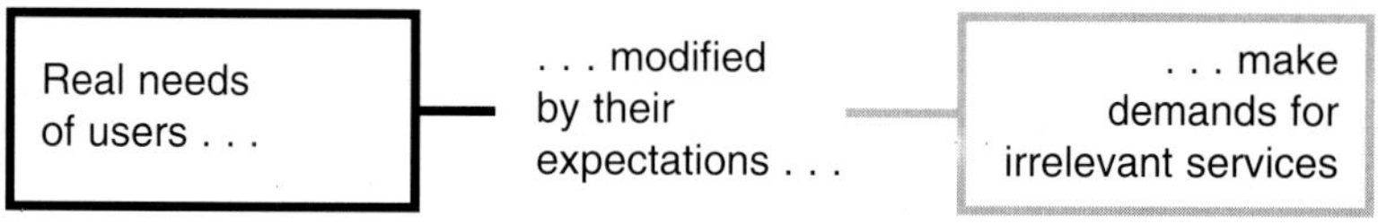

and like this if you look at the librarian:

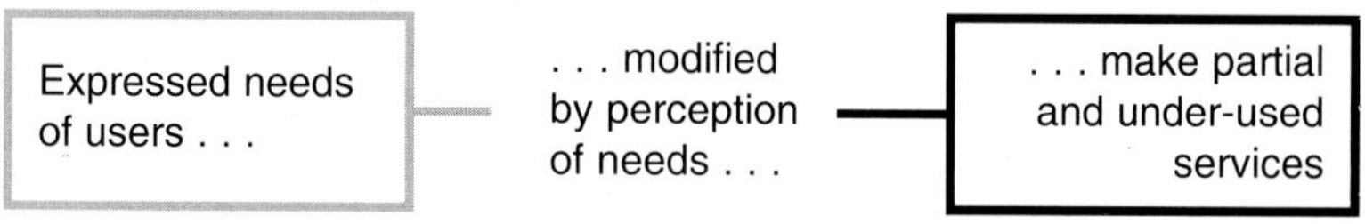

These pictures remain true if neither side takes action: the user, to express needs more clearly; and the librarian to be problem— and not resource—orientated.

The most common plea that we get from users when we carry out needs analysis is for the library staff to learn about what the branches, divisions and other groupings do. Their most common experience is that library staff will talk about, and advertise, the *resources* that can be deployed. Unfortunately most users think in terms of their *problems* and what they want to hear is answers, not products that may be sources of answers.

A typical example of this sort of thing is the situation we found a few years ago when looking at a group of laboratories. On behalf of their scientific staff, the information unit spent a healthy five-figure sum each year generating a current-awareness bulletin. It was printed on glossy art paper and took three electronic transformations (database to word processor to desktop publishing) to prepare. The citations in it were often six months old by the time it was published, and what readers got was a series of bibliographic references. What they needed, and very badly, was a comprehensive subject-based SDI service delivered ultra-fast to their laboratory benches.

Another sort of disjunction was a user satisfaction survey that we found being conducted as a regular activity by a library. This asked users to rank their satisfaction with library services. The services were all expressed in terms of processes such as inter-library loans, journal circulation and book loans. Respondents were asked to indicate their degree of satisfaction with these things. The problem here was two-fold. Nowhere were they asked whether they wanted or needed these things or even knew what they were; nor were they asked what kind of service they really needed. Despite this the responses were collated and counted and a satisfaction index computed which was reported to senior management as a performance measure.

Analysing the problem. One of the basic tools for the analysis of users needs is a deceptively simple matrix. On this you plot defined user groups; and services provided to them. In the cells of the matrix, where user group and service coincide, you note how that service supports the group. The support may be a figure showing, for instance, the number of article copies supplied. A typical matrix looks like the example on page 47.

The first attempt at such a matrix will almost certainly produce a list of *processes* down the left-hand column, and a list of operational groups across the top. Neither of these will yield very much real

	Policy group A	HRD	IT & IS		
Book loans	27	18	14		
Journal circulation	5	8	2		
Online searches	7	3	2		
Press cuttings	6	6	1		

information. The reasons are that the processes are not in themselves reasons why things are done; and the operational groupings do not express how services are used. The numbers in the cells represent nothing much more than a count of transactions, and do not indicate the significance of the transactions at all. Far too many library statistics look just like this. They are useful for planning

	Marketing	Financial control	Research		
Current awareness					
Text of journal articles					
Market and competitor analyses					
Retrospective legislation					

workload and staffing patterns but they are no use as business planning and development tools because they do not show whether the activities are meaningful or purposeful.

The second attempt should remedy the shortcomings of the first. Probably there will be no numbers in it. Turn the matrix inside out and try plotting some generic service types down the left side, and the reasons why people might draw on them across the top. You will find rather different activities and clumps of users coming out, when you plot *purposes* against types of use:

Now you are plotting *how* information is used (eg for marketing) against *types* of information. Note that no mention is made of how the information is delivered. That is what you start to put in to the cells of the matrix. This approach gets away from the process-bound viewpoint. It also recognises that within any operational grouping (be it a division or a branch) there are people doing a variety of different jobs. The horizontal axis picks these up. It is, however, necessary to understand two vey important things about the horizontal axis:

- Words like "Research" and "Marketing" are not job titles; they are the circumstances in which some people may work some of the time. So any information-analysing and collating activity is research;

- anybody in the organisation may be carrying out any one of these activities at any time—they are not job-specific and are not grade-related.

Into each cell you write details of how that sort of activity is performed (if it is) for a chosen type of usage.

Using the matrix. Really there should be two goes made at this: the first is to plot what is happening now; and the second is to plot what should be happening.

What is happening will be informed by using the matrix to examine the work of various user groups. Take them one at a time, and do not try to be too ambitious. Choose a group such as "Division A". Then in consultation with the group, determine all the marketing activities that go on. These will include things like preparing literature for internal and external consumption; or seeking opportunities for the Division to work in collaboration with others. Look hard and critically at how the library functions support each activity, and enter the result on the matrix. Do the same for other activities like research and financial control.

For what should be happening, ask of each cell the simple question "why?" In other words, should this happen, in this way, at this volume? The "why?" question cannot be asked or answered without having formulated some sort of a mission statement for the library because part of the question is about whether the activity supports that mission. This second version of the matrix should demonstrate how the mission is achieved.

At its crudest if the mission of the library is to support policy-making divisions in HQ with externally-published documentation, then the loan of books to the IT support unit is an obvious activity to stop. Similarly providing ILL in an area where overwhelmingly the need is for current awareness and press alerting seems to indicate a total mismatch of requirements and services.

The mission statement supplies the context for understanding. The "what is happening now" version of the matrix is the baseline for evaluating the extent to which the mission is being achieved. Overlying that matrix with the "what should be happening"one shows the extent to which corrective action needs to be taken. Of course it is possible that it will just show that the mission statement was badly expressed, or plain wrong. At least now you have the tools to analyse the present and plan the future.

The information audit. A financial audit is about establishing whether cash flowing in and out of some defined area of business has been accounted for adequately. Unpack that a little. Firstly it does not mean whether the money was spent to good effect, or whether it was spent appropriately. It is fair to say that if the till had been emptied by a thief then provided the thief left a note indicating exactly how much had been stolen, the auditors would be satisfied. Of course they might have something to say to management about security, but that is beside the point. It is the accountability (the extent to which the cash flow is documented) that is at issue. Secondly it is important to choose the area of business. To measure the whole of an activity against the whole of its parent organisation is a task doomed to become bogged down in an intractable morass of unreconcilable data. It is preferable to choose one functional area of service at a time, and then concentrate on understanding its nature.

An information audit is a different matter, as it looks at things the other way round. Given a cost for a resource, how has it been deployed? Over the life of the information contained in the resource, how has that been used? Please be careful here to distinguish between simple counts of activity (so many books lent out over such a period) and trying to measure the effectiveness on the user of each of those loans. An information audit is about purpose, not process. Purposes are expresed in terms of the wider business activities that they support; processes in terms of what has to be done to achieve the purposes.

The field of the information audit does not ignore cost, but tries to take it in to account as only one factor. Information is "soft" in the sense that cost is quite easy to establish, but benefit is not. Cost can be quantified (hence the budget exercise) but benefit gained or lost is largely a non-numeric measure and so conventional accounting leaves it out altogether. You can see this in the development of a business case for new systems. Actual costs are derived and projected; benefits are expressed in terms of better working, integrated access *etc.* We are very poorly served in our profession with the means to evaluate non-numeric measures of performance.

There is no one magic method of carrying out an audit. There is certainly no almighty algorithm into which all figures are plugged, and out of which plops a single answer. What there is is a range of techniques that can be used to develop an understanding of elements of the problem. Skill and professional judgement supply the context. There are three things that need to be understood as being in an interlinked relationship: the mission of the overall

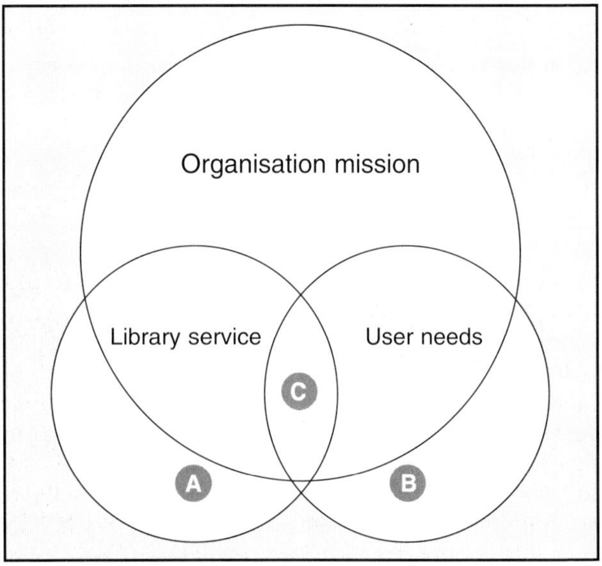

Figure 1: inter-relationship of mission, needs and services

organisation; the objectives of the users in the area under consideration; and the library service in its widest sense (staff, stock, services, processes) as it applies to those users. An idealised picture looks something like this:

In reality one or more of the circles is distorted at the expense of the others. There are several things that you are trying to spot in an audit:

- Does area (A) lie wholly within the circle defining the total organisation? (This can only be true if there is no interaction by this library with other organisations, through ILL or networking—an unusual and unhealthy situation);
- Does area (B) lie wholly within the circle defining the total organisation? (Possible, if it is an internal service function, but this needs to be understood);
- If all functions within the total organisation are plotted, is area (C) the same size as the circle of library services? It should be.

If you find situations where one circle is bloated at the expense of the others; or where each circle overlaps only one other, then there is something seriously wrong with either the analysis or the organisation (or both).

An information audit can use a version of the matrix idea to illustrate the analysis of user needs. User needs are one of the main inputs to the audit. Provided they are expressed as kinds of information and not kinds of resources, they make an effective starting point. In Figure 2 the left-hand column is a range of needs expressed by users. The horizontal axis covers the six locations in which the users were found. A tick shows whether or not that service was required by anyone at that location. The needs are those that were volunteered to us, without any guidance as to what was or was not available. In the same manner as with the earlier matrices, this one needs an alternative version, to show what the situation should be. And here a critical problem becomes apparent. The difference between what is and what should be indicates the extent to which the library is seen by users as an effective organisation that has something to offer them. The matrix has some spaces where there should be ticks, and *vice versa*. It is a picture of a library service that is unaware of user needs, unlikely to find them out, and content to try

Figure 2: User-specified requirements by site

	Site A	Site B	Site C	Site D	Site E	Site F
Hansard: (Lords, Commons, Standing committees, PQs etc.) current and past	✓	✓	✓	✓	✓	
Reference texts: core reference works in the major areas of interest – current editions	✓		✓	✓	✓	✓
Departmental publications: this and other relevant Departments	✓	✓	✓	✓	✓	
Purposeful acquisition: active acquisition of material in advance of requests for it	✓	✓	✓			✓
Active dissemination: alerting users to relevant material	✓	✓	✓	✓		
Legislation: retrospective	✓	✓	✓			✓
Maps and travel information	✓	✓		✓	✓	
Early warning on external issues and publications	✓	✓	✓			
Networked catalogue access	✓		✓	✓		
Press cuttings/news alerting	✓	✓		✓		
Internal document series: circulars, press notices etc.	✓	✓				✓
Book loans	✓		✓	✓		
Internal/external liaison and networking to appropriate information services and sources	✓		✓	✓		
External database services	✓	✓				✓
Current awareness and alerting	✓	✓				
'Grey' literature: publications of pressure groups and research bodies	✓	✓				
Research reports collection	✓					✓
Exploitation of information: an active library service that makes its collection work	✓					✓
CPD training material	✓			✓		
Browsing access	✓					✓
Totals	**20**	**12**	**10**	**10**	**4**	**8**

and help if it can, but only when asked. Thus the use of this particular baseline for an audit will show a very poor correlation between requirements and resources.

The second input to the process is the resources. As before there are two routes from which to choose: the resources actually available; and those that could be made available.

The process of analysing either of these routes is broadly similar. It is to map, or plot, the contents and means of delivery over the requirements. That is easily said, but not so easily done. In practice the outcome of the analysis is a series of subjective statements about needs and resources backed up with specific examples. This should not be surprising given my earlier statements about the differences between a financial audit and an information one.

The understanding of resources is a complicated area. Take the example of access to proceedings of the House. *Hansard, Justis Parliamentary* and the Chadwyck-Healey product are all obvious contenders, but each has particular strengths and weaknesses in terms of coverage. The means of technical delivery are also different. The library has just one of these to meet all levels and types of need. How do you relate its suitability to user requirements?

Look at what users are saying about expected frequency of access, the need for immediate or delayed access, and for how far back coverage is required. Different groups will have quite different packages of requirements, and it will be necessary to analyse each in turn. Take the existing product and establish how it matches each individual criterion. It may be possible to use some sort of scoring system to show the extent to which the resource meets each criterion.

It will be no great surprise to find that each user group that has identified a need for the same resource is unlikely to be satisfied by the one and only offering of it that the library has. The uncomfortable outcome may be that all three products are required. This presupposes that it has been established that the user needs have been found to fall within the mission statement. Obviously you only evaluate requirements that are within that.

Using the results of an audit to plan future service provision is really only an extension of the same thinking. Let us assume for example that a constraint is that there can be no networked access by users to online or CD-ROM sources. That still means that all three services can be used by the library on behalf of users. The critical factors can be tabulated for each product and the extent of the "fit" analysed to see what matches best. An analysis that we carried out for the laboratories mentioned earlier examined each of 24 specialist databases available to the scientists to support their work. Through a series of interviews followed up by checklist questionnaires we asked over 100 of the scientists to tell us about their needs for information types. Each type was to be scored ranking its importance to the individual on a four-step scale from "high" to "low", frequency of requirement on a four-step scale from "continually" to "never", and delivery via self-service arrangements, or through an information intermediary.

We used the criteria of currency (how up to date) and coverage (how extensive) to graph a rectangle that described each database. Then over the graph we plotted another rectangle that showed

Figure 3: Service provision and user requirement plotted jointly

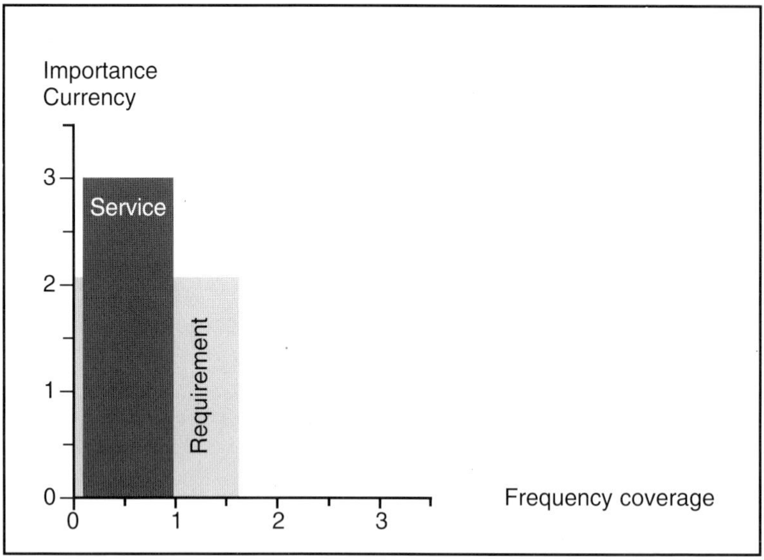

importance against frequency, on the same scale. The result was 24 graphs (Figure 3 is an example of one) demonstrating the extent to which what was provided met what was needed. The results were, for the most part, quite alarming.

This approach worked very well for its particular circumstance, but the method might be suspect in other cases, which simply illustrates that point that the outcome of an information audit is the analysis of evidence, and not the end-product of a set of fixed techniques.

Putting it all together. All of the components are now in place for getting a good 'handle' on the LIS business, so it is worth finishing with a few notes of warning:

- statements of user needs are only as good as the questions asked;
- analysis of those needs must be done with care and understanding;
- information audits are mostly qualitative and not quantitative, and there are no simple numbers that say "good" or "bad";
- an audit involves applying a range of techniques, the results of which will aid understanding'
- most important of all—do not confuse transaction volumes with measures of effectiveness, because they are only counts of processes, and do not explain purposes.

What I Want from a Library Service

Patricia Stoat

Small Firms and Business Link, DTI

When I was asked to speak to you today about a user view of the virtual library, my reaction was: what is a virtual library? How would I recognise one? It seemed that my task was not to worry about such things but to use my imagination—the virtual library could be, well, virtually anything I wanted it to be.

It must have been obvious when printed books first appeared that the end of the library was in sight. There were only so many books in the world—already, no doubt, too many, in the views of more conservative commentators; there was only so much to be known, and only so many people capable of writing with wit, elegance and style. Soon it would be possible for that small group of people with the ability to read and sufficient leisure to do so to own all the books they might desire. Everything they could possiby want to know would be there, at the turm of a page, on their own bookshelves. The library was finished. Librarianship had no future.

It did not, of course, work out quite like that. Print material multiplied exceedingly, until it seemed likely that all the forests in the world would be insufficient to provide the paper to keep it going. The more people were able to buy books, the more they used libraries, and the more they depended upon the skills of librarians to help them surf the tidal waves of print without being overwhelmed. Librarians became, and remain, masters of document management and control. If I want a document, and I know what it is—any significant feature which will identify it—I am very confident that you, as librarians, will be able to find it for me. The consequence of this is, that I take this service of the library for granted. I am not impressed when you succeed in identifying and obtaining for me the book, the journal article, the British Standard or German patent that I want; merely irritated if you do not. *You* know how much thought and care has gone into creating your catalogues; how much intellectual endeavour into devising classification systems which model the real world; how much management skill is required to maintain stocks of millions of items accessed by thousands of borrowers. I not only do not know these things, I am not really very interested. I know what I want—and these days it is quite often not a document at all.

I do not necessarily distinguish between documents and other kinds of information media:

- did I read this in the paper, or hear it on the Today programme?

- is it UK legislation, or an EU proposal?

I do not want you to ask me these things—I want you to tell me. I think that the real point is that I use the library less as a source of documents, and still less as a source of information about documents; much more as a source of knowledge, or of the sources of knowledge in its many varieties.

The user of the virtual library is already accustomed to shopping in Sainsbury's. This experience is a defining one in contemporary urban life. If I am planning a dinner party, and am shopping on Saturday morning with a delightful day of creative cooking to look forward to, the supermarket offers me a range of fresh ingredients, of every kind. If I am rushed and hurried on a weekday evening, with guests expected and nothing prepared, it offers ready made meals, even gourmet meals, of every kind. In between, the supermarket offers components in various stages of preparation to suit my needs: frozen puff pastry, real mayonnaise, ready-washed salads. Someone at Sainsbury's has done a lot of thinking, not just about what I need, but about the variety of needs that I have, and has developed systems and services that offer me more than choice—choices, as it were, about choice.

The car industry offers another instance of the steps towards the virtual experience that should characterise the virtual library. Within the decade (if what they say is true) we will see the end of the Ford era—"you can have your model-T any colour you like, so long as it's black"—and the dawn of the age of customised mass production. When we buy new cars in the future we will use sophisticated software in the car showroom to select and design exactly the features we want: engine size, type of gearbox, type of CD player, size of sunroof. The dealer will transmit the design to the factory, and three days later the car will be delivered, to your personal specification. It seems to me that this will have interesting implications for the actual manufacturing side of the car business: will there be thousands of small, highly automated, manufacturing plants building customised products for lots of different manufacturers all around the world? If not, how will they achieve the delivery times? For, of course, when I have designed my customised Escort, as a good post-modern customer, I will want it now.

This brings me closer to what I mean by "virtual". It seems to mean:

- customised;
- available when I want it;
- user friendly;
- offering "choice about choice"
- the ingredients for soup (data);
- the components for soup—stock cubes, prepared vegetables (information);
- ready made soup (knowledge).

The *customised* library is the information/knowledge base which is designed to meet my requirements, to understand me. It will need detailed records of what I have read, and what I am interested in. It will know my habits, tastes, characteristics, preferences, intellectual history. It will be designed to use this information to modify requests that I make, cross check its own advice, help me to clarify my thinking:

- find me an English country house detective story that I have not read in the last three years;
- find me the article in the Financial Times last month which argued that redistributive taxation is a form of theft;
- find me some statistics on how many people who join the Internet do not rejoin when their first subscription runs out.

The *readily available* library is the library that I can use when I need to, whether this is at the busiest time of day when all telephone lines are engaged and long lines of people wait at issue desks, or at 2am—like many open learning students, this is the time I really need to access the library! Or when I am in the bath.

The *user friendly* library is one which understands its own collections and resources in the terms in which I want to access them:

- I have to go to a meeting on a subject (say, virtual libraries) of which I know nothing—I need a short, non technical article to give me a general overview of the subject;
- I have to give a talk on the use of case based expert systems in business information units—I need a recent review article or something similar to update me on the current state of the art;
- I need to understand the difference between the US and EU approaches to the law on consumer protection: is there a short book available that's up-to-date and authoritative?

The *options and choices* library will be able to help the user to find data, information, or knowledge, to skip between these different kinds of resource, and to understand the connections between them. It will be not just a learning or research resource, but also a teaching and mentoring device for its users.

You will note that I have been talking about the library, and not about librarians. This does not mean that the virtual library will not need librarians: it will need librarians more highly skilled and competent than ever. But so far as the user, contacting the library remotely with what ever tools are to hand, is concerned, it is with the library as an organic system that contact will take place. To the librarian, designing and managing this extraordinary device, the user will be as virtual as the library.

How do you go about designing a library for the virtual user? Cataloguing becomes a more sophisticated art, blacker than ever and more vital. The library will need to know everything that a user might want to know about every item contained within the library, and all the connections between them. Hypertext will link text, footnotes, citations, reviews, across disciplines, languages and periods. Classification must develop to mirror not reality but the "realities" of virtual groups of users, and of individual users, so that navigation across cultures and universes of knowledge which have been closed becomes feasible, even easy. Systems design and maintenance, and the imaginative development of the interactive, organic, qualities of the library, will be essential skills for the keeper of the virtual library. Its going to be an exciting time to be a librarian, the information age.

Who wants, or needs, the virtual library? Will the library I've described ever be a resource generally available to everyone, something one takes for granted as one takes the public library for granted? In the library world, information technology has been used more to achieve economies of scale, to keep staffing levels down, reduce costs and automate procedures than it has to facilitate and improve customer service. In supermarkets, by way of contrast, similar technologies and techniques have been employed for similar purposes, but with an eye always on making shopping a more "life enhancing experience" for the customer. This may be a result of competitive pressures: there is always another supermarket to try. May we expect in future a world of competing libraries, subscription based, offering ever-improving levels of access, intuitive searching, speed and user support?

My guess is that we will.

Beyond the OPAC: delivering intelligence over the network

David Smith
Department of Health

In the summer of 1991 the Department of Health submitted a business case to the Treasury for an Office Information System (OIS), and approval was given in Autumn 1991. The business case defined an IT and support infrastructure to provide a Department-wide office automation system and to build a consistent IT base on which future applications could be developed.

The two year installation programme was to provide all of the, then, 3,800 Departmental staff with training and access to wordprocessing and electronic mail. This was to be achieved through a coherent network of PCS, at a ratio of about 80% PCS to staff. Existing IT applications would be retained snd, where possible, integrated into the OIS network. The OIS programme was to establish a support infrastructure to manage the network on an ongoing basis.

The Business Case benefits were linked to the relocation of about 1,000 civil servants in what is now the NHS Executive to Leeds. This included savings on post and telecommunications, but more importantly, OIS was a key enabler of the relocation. The use of electronic mail for rapid transfer of documents from London to Leeds would allow Departmental business to continue despite the 200 mile separation of the NHS Executive from Private Office and the London-based policy groups. Supplemented by video conferencing facilities, OIS was installed in the DH estate over 24 months, which is a very short timescale considering the number of staff to be networked, and the fact that a number of them were in the process of moving to another part of the country.

By March 1994 every division inthe Department had been provided with OIS. Implementation has included the rollout of local and wide-area networks, training programmes and setting up a support infrastructure. There are more than 4,000 registered users of the OIS network located mainly in London and Leeds. Although this number will reduce by approximately 700 staff by July 1996, this will be more than made up for by the addition of 1,000 staff in 8 Departmental Regional Offices following on from the reorganisation of the NHS and the removal of Regional Health Authorities.

Technical overview. OIS is linked by ethernet Local Area Networks (LANS) within buildings, and between buildings via a router Wide Area Network (WAN). It provides a basic physical network infrastructure, a server platform of approximately 90 Netware 3.11 servers, standard character-based workstations, location independant access via a standard menu interface, a standard WP facility, E-mail and access, including terminal emulation to a number of existing host computers including a Prime minicomputer, Amdahl mainframe, ICL mainframe and various Unix systems. Initially installed with a DOS desktop, users are now being converted to a Windows 3.1 environment (known as OIS2), with currently 40% of users converted. OIS2 provides a number of standard applications:

- Wordperfect 5.2+ for wordprocessing;
- Route400 for e-mail facilities;
- Lotus 1-2-3 for spreadsheets;
- Lotus Approach for personal databases;
- Freelance Graphics for presentations.

In addition, individual users (or groups of users) have access to a variety of non-standard products including Lotus Symphony and Paradox for specific legacy systems. PC workstations include Compaq and Siemens-Nixdorf 386 and 486 based PCS, with a minimum configuration of 4MB RAM and 40 MB HD, VGA colour screens and network cards. This specification is gradually being upgraded to

Pentiums with 8 MB RAM and 340MB disks. OIS servers (Intel, Compaq, Siemens-Nixdorf) are configured to a standaed specification, each including at least 486 processor, 32MB RAM, 4GB of disk storage and DAT tape drive for automatic overnight backup. Each user has access to a nearby network laser printer (HP Laserjet 3 or 4).

Building LANS use 10 Base T ethernet transport mechanisms, with 100 Mbit/s FDDI rings linking floors in the buildings serving larger user populations. Links to host computers, including the Department's Prime, use TCP/IP. The WAN backbone consists of high speed leased circuits linking resilient dual operational routers in five main buildings. Other sites are connected by site routers and leased bearers.

Document and Information Management Strategy. One consequence of the short installation timescale imposed by the Leeds move was that considerations of the use of OIS as a means of disseminating corporate information were left to later, while the more immediate requirements of training and supporting users in using wordprocessing and e-mail facilities took priority. In 1993 DH's Information Services Directorate, which encompasses the DH's computer services sections as well as library services and Departmental records, issued a Document and Information Management Strategy (DIMS) paper which was approved by the Departmental Information Strategy Steering Committee. DIMS recommended the development of appropriate policies, procedures and systems for document management, as well as the development of corporate sources of information using the existing OIS infrastructure. DIMS proposed a number of initiatives to improve the management of information and documents both on OIS and in the Department generally. The strategy addressed a number of areas/issues:

- management of the proliferating number of electronic documents in existence;
- alternative ways of distributing electronic information, other than by email;
- use of various technologies and techniques to deliver and handle information , including text retrieval, Departmental thesauri, and CDROMS.

The management of electronic and paper based documents and records was met with a Document Management Initiative within DH, and is being carried out over a 2 year timescale. This initiative, although originating from early DIMS work, is now being carried forward by the Departmental Records Section. Alternative ways of distributing information, or intelligence, to the desktop and the use of various technologies to do so were addressed by the development of a number of DIMS networked information services.

Networked Information Services. DIMS proposed a number of ways of reducing the number of documents being stored on the system, and of making greater use of the networking opportunities OIS offered to disseminate information. One of these was the development of information services over the network. These would seek to speed up the amount of routine information distributed across the Department, and to offer a more disk capacity efficient alternative to using purely large scale email distributions. Before detailing the services that have been, and are being, developed, it is worth noting a number of common principles that underlie them.

DIMS information services principles.

- DIMS projects currently use only existing technology already available on OIS, (eg Wordperfect, Microsoft Windows). This has meant that current awareness services such as the Press Index Service and the Hansard Summary are using Wordperfect as the means of information delivery. A DIMS Notice Board, which provides electronic access to Departmental reference information such as T&S rate, uses the Microsoft Windows Help agent.

- DIMS project costs should be kept to a minimum. This has partly been achieved by using the software already in use by DH staff, thereby cutting training and capital costs for the projects. Transmission and access methods have been kept very simple so that additional programming costs are kept to a minimum. It has also meant that the Divisions responsible for creating and distributing the information, for example Information Division, can easily operate the system without costly support from ISD (eg DIMS Noticeboard).

- in line with reducing development costs, the technical design for projects (eg Press Index and Hansard service) has been duplicated wherever possible. This "boiler plating" approach to DIMS projects is aimed at cutting down development costs by reusing tried and proven technology and design wherever possible, and the reduction of "leading edge" practice.

- benefits identified for the DIMS information services must include cash releasing savings, not just nominal benefits such as better informed staff. Cash releasing savings for the Press Index are half an administration officer and £12,000 in the print budget, and for the Hansard Index £18,000 will be saved in daily Hansard subscriptions in the first year of operation.
- information services, thus far, have been delivered to the desktop of all staff. This has reduced support costs in carrying out a selective rollout and the need for the access rights of a number of users to be continually updated as they change posts within the Department, or as new users join or existing users leave.
- the services developed be capable of operation by end users with the minimum training—in most cases by the distribution of printed instructions.

Given these principles, a number of information services have been developed by DIMS and these are described in more detail.

Staff Location Database. A precedent for this already existed on OIS, as the Department's formerly paper based internal telephone directory, the Staff Location Directory, had been transferred to OIS and could be accessed using a simple front end. The data for this was distributed overnight to the file servers that supported the IS user population, and staff accessed this data from a common location on their local file server. By distributing the data in this way, ISD avoided the need for heavy traffic across the WAN accessing one single common point. The total size of data was comparatively small for the SLD; indeed it can be accessed as a TSR running within approximately 32K of RAM.

Press Index Service. A project was set up with the objectives of providing all DH staff with daily access to two files: one of the daily Press Summary and one of the DH Press Notices, both issued daily by the Department's Information Division the press headlines of interest to the DH, and the other the full text of DH Press Releases. This was achieved by having the two files prepared by Information Division, who receive the Press Summary electronically from an external source and who hold their Press Releases electronically anyway. The actual files contain one week's coverage of Press Summaries and Press Notices, and can be easily scrolled through using WordPerfect. Access to the service is via an INFORMATION option on the top level OIS menu for DOS users, or a Press Index Service icon within an INFORMATION group for Windows users.

Hansard Summary Service. A PRINCE methodology was employed to run the project, in common with most DH run IT projects. In order to get the fullest utility form this process, in terms of technical design and quality assurance DIMS seeks to "boiler plate" as much as possible, ensuring that experience gained from past DIMS projects is brought to bear in future ones. In the case of the daily Hansard Summary Index Service project, the same basic technical design was used as the Press Index Summary, with two WordPerfect files updated daily, listing debates and parliamentary questions of relevance to DH from the most recent Hansard; one file covering House of Commons Hansard, the other Lords. One enhancement to this service, compared to the Press Summary, was the addition of an automated document ordering service, enabling users to identify items of interest and email details of their request directly to the library.

Unlike the Press Summary, where savings derived largely from efficiency gains, the Hansard Service derived its savings from reductions in the library's overall expenditure on daily Hansard. The ability to provide on demand hardcopy over OIS is a further development that is desirable for both the Press and Hansard services, but the issues involved in storing and transmitting scanned images, to say nothing of copyright, still need to be addressed.

Distribution of Business. This is DH's internal directory of who does what in the Department; OGDs will have similar publications carrying out the same function. Using the same technology as was used for the SLD, the DOB was made available to users in early 1995. One problem that did face ISD in developing this as an electronic service, was incorporating the user demand for a thesaurus to help navigate round parts of the Department's work unfamiliar to most staff. Coincidentally an 18,000 term Departmental Standarf Thesaurus, also one of the DIMS recommendations,was completed in February 1994 and it was decided to interface this with the DOB.

The result has been a thesaurus "option" which can be turned on or off when using the DOB, but which can otherwise be completely transparent to the user. This allows the user to enter a non-preferred term, but to automatically retrieve sections that are described using the preferred term linked to it. Where a term is retrieved through the thesaurus it is highlighted in grey. The thesaurus is also useful in "translating" abbreviations that are used in describing the work of the Department. The thesaurus is run against the text of the DOB each day, and any terms in the thesaurus not linked to the text in the DOB are removed. The result is that users search a "sub-thesaurus", which contains terms that will alwasys result in a retrieved section(s) if entered.

DIMS Noticeboard. While earlier DIMS projects had concentrated on focused areas of comparatively volatile information, there remained a need to provide a mechanism to mount relatively stable Departmental "reference" type information, without the need to go through an elaborate IT project each time an additional information resource needed to be added. In addressing this need, DIMS was also seeking to identify a cost-effective solution that utilised existing networked software. At this time the Department started to migrate from a predominantly DOS based system to Microsoft Windows based ine, and this offered a new basis for designing such an information facility.

Using the Windows' Help agent, a DIMS Noticeboard was built which enable discrete pieces of information to be presented to the user, linked by pseudo-hypertext links and offering printing facilities. There are limitations with this approach; it is not possible to alert users to the fact that information has been updated on the Noticeboard, and so is not suitable to time-critical information services such as current awareness. Nevertheless, for reference-type material such as current transport and subsistence rates, Departmental abbreviations and addresses, and for irregular in-house publications, it has proved a cost-effective and network-stable solution.

Conclusion. Particular importance has placed upon continual communication between the DIMS team and user groups before, during and after implementation — and this has paid great dividends in the ease of installation and acceptance. A wide range of support skills, tools and procedures have been developed. Management of the OIS network is continually being improved, and it is now operating well within the performance parameters desired. The Department has successfully made a substantial "step change" — not just in the IT equipment and software installed, but also in the overall level of skill and usage of office automation, and in the absorbtion of IT into working processes. Continued support and incremental improvement of the system is assured, and will continue to be built upon.

Printed in the United Kingdom for The Stationery Office
Dd 302490 5/97 10170 559/4